Let Me Tell You About My Baby

Let Me Tell You About My Baby

Story and Pictures by

Roslyn Banish

A Harper Trophy Book

Harper & Row, Publishers

Let Me Tell You About My Baby
Copyright © 1982 by Roslyn Banish
Originally published under the title
I Want to Tell You About My Baby
by Wingbow Press, Berkeley, California.
Printed in the United States of America. All rights reserved.
Typography by Andrew Rhodes
First Harper Trophy edition, 1988.

Library of Congress Cataloging-in-Publication Data
Banish, Roslyn, date
  [I want to tell you about my baby]
  Let me tell you about my baby / story and pictures by Roslyn
Banish.
      p.   cm.
  Previously published as: I want to tell you about my baby.
  Summary: A little boy explains his mother's pregnancy, the
birth of the baby, the care that it needs, and his feelings about his
new brother.
  ISBN 0-06-020382-X : $.   ISBN 0-06-020383-8
(lib. bdg.) : $.   ISBN 0-06-446084-3 (pbk.) : $
  1. Infants—Juvenile literature.   2. Pregnancy—Juvenile
literature.   3. Childbirth—Juvenile literature.   4. Brothers and
sisters—Juvenile literature.   [1. Pregnancy.   2. Childbirth.
3. Babies.   4. Brothers and sisters.]   I. Title.
HQ774.B32 1988   *87-31890*
306.8′7—dc19   *CIP*
                                                               AC

To Andrew Wolf Epstein

Very special thanks to the Flack Family:
Betsy and Jim, Andrew and Bardin, and Betsy's parents,
Beulah and Fran Hodge.

The medical photographs were assisted by
Christa Williams R.N., Director, FAMCAP,
Leon Zdan, M.D., Richard Topel, M.D.,
all of Kaiser-Permanente Medical Center,
San Francisco. The photograph on page 20
was done by Dirk Schenkkan.

Let Me Tell You About My Baby

That's my Mom and Dad and me.
There's a baby growing inside my Mom.
We have bread to feed the ducks.

My Mom can't pick me up anymore.
The baby is too big.
She can't even button her jacket.
Dad picks me up and holds me upside down.
I love it.

Mom is reading a story to me.
I can't sit on her lap anymore.
She is too bumpy.

But we still snuggle.
That's me talking to the baby. "Hi baby."
The baby doesn't answer.

My Mom lets me touch her big belly.
Sometimes I feel the baby move. It feels funny.
My Mom says the baby gets bigger every day.

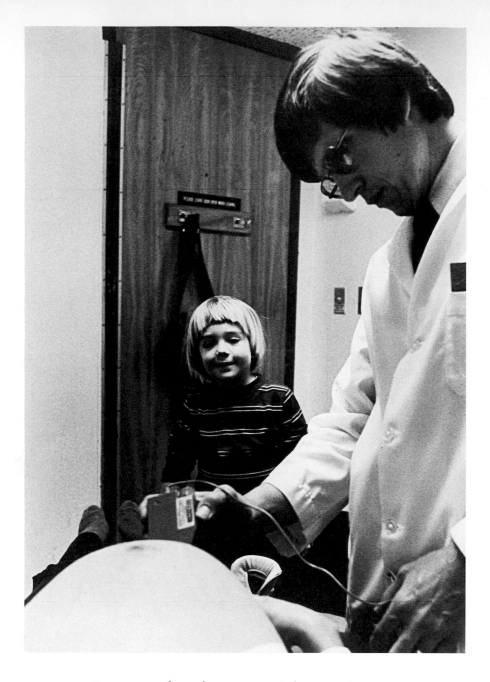

I go to the doctor with my Mom.
He listens to the baby's heartbeat
with a special radio. The doctor
says we have to wait some more.
I don't like waiting for the baby.

My Mom is tired all the time.
The baby makes her sleepy.
I want her to play with me like she used to.

I look at a book all by myself. It's about ships.
I love ships and dinosaurs and spaceships and
Batman and Superman and oatmeal cookies with raisins.

We're doing exercises. I am wearing my Superman tights.
My Mom has to get strong so she can push the baby out.
I am strong because I am Superman.
My Dad exercises with us.

My Dad and I are getting the baby's room ready.
He tells me this little bed was mine when I was a baby.
Now I am a big boy. I have a BIG bed.

I don't remember when I was a baby.
My Dad shows me my baby pictures.
Boy, do I look funny!

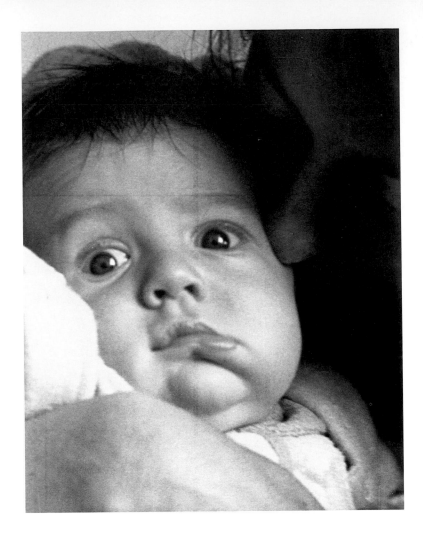

This is me when I was a baby.

That's my Grandma and Grandpa.
They are going to take care of me when the
baby comes. We do fun things together.

One day my Mom tells me the baby is ready to be born.
Hooray! No more waiting.
My Mom packs her bag. She and my Dad go to the hospital.

I stay home with my Grandma and Grandpa.
We make oatmeal cookies with raisins.
When will my Mom come home?
I miss her.

Grandma sews an *S* on my Superman cape.

I think about Superman and my Mom.

My Mom is in this hospital.
Here she is waiting for the baby to be born.

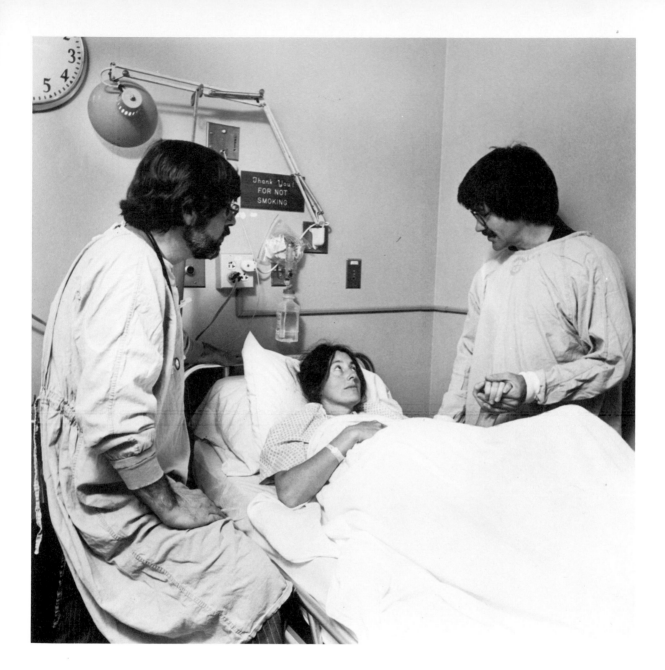

The man with my Dad is the doctor.
He is going to help my Mom.
It's hard work for my Mom, and it takes a long time.
But my Dad is always there.

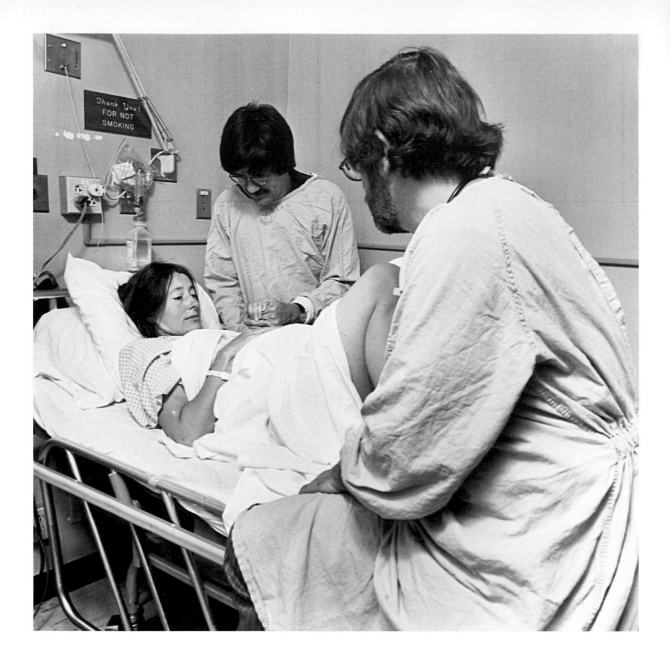

Finally my Mom gives a big push.
The baby comes out an opening between her legs.
My Dad says that is how I was born too.
The doctor catches it and says it's a boy.

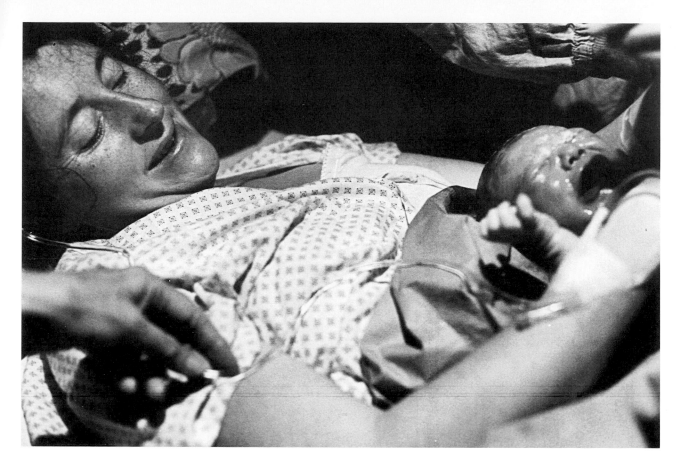

That means I have a brother.

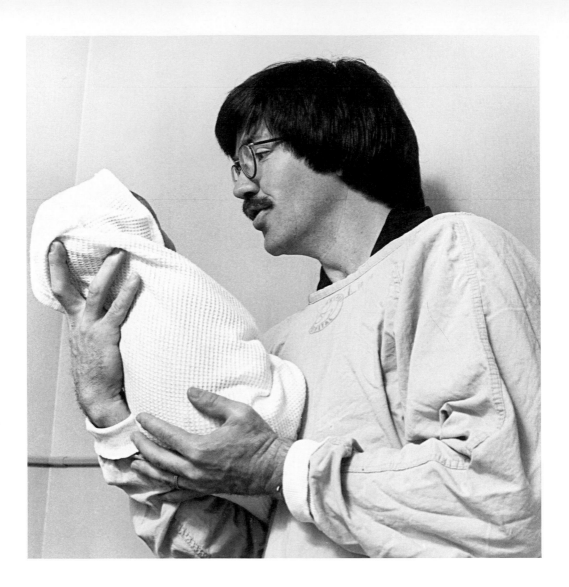

They wrap up the baby to keep him warm.

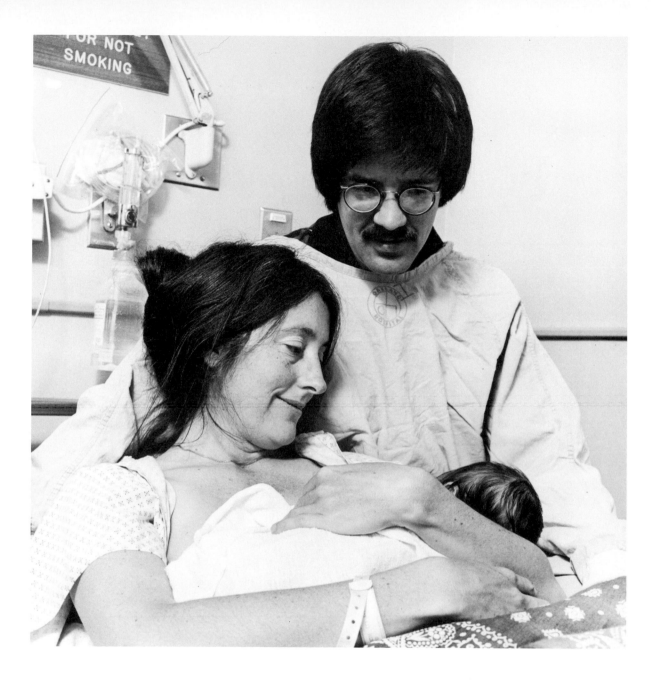

Then they give him a big hug.

My Grandpa takes me to the hospital.
Here I'm waiting to see the baby.
Where is my Mom? Where is my Dad?
Where is the baby?

Here she is!
My Mom gives me a great big hug
and says "I love you."
I tell her to come home.
Where's the baby?

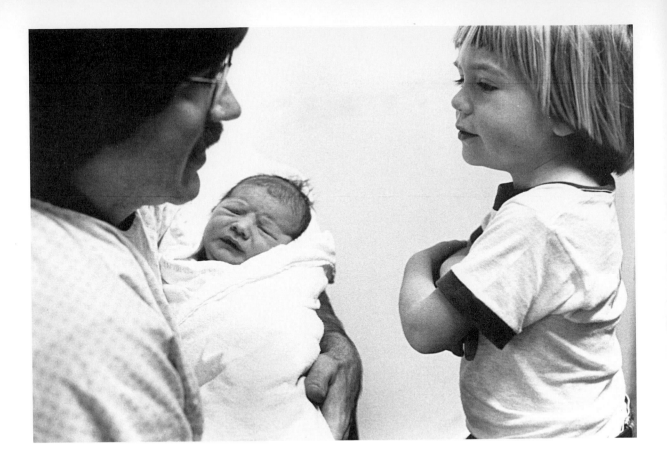

My Dad shows the baby to me.

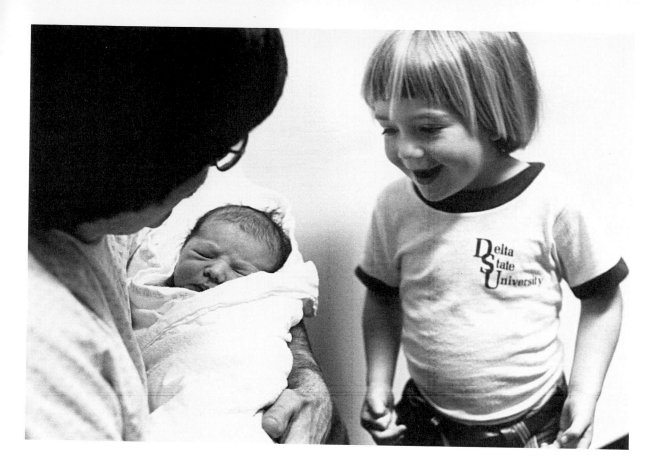

He is so little and has lots of wrinkles.

My Mom and the baby stay in the hospital
a few days to rest. Finally my Dad goes
to bring them home.
Yeah! Here they are!

I get a big hug.

The baby is home now but I can't play with him.
He just wants to sleep...

and cry . . .

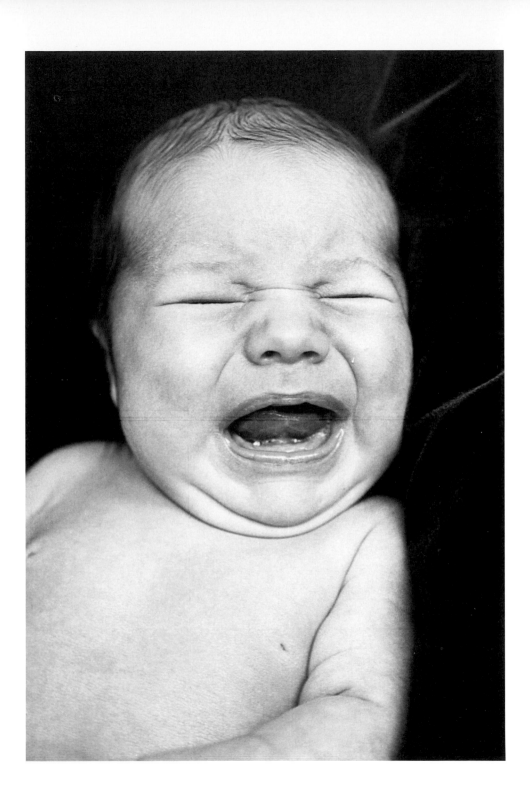

and eat.
Here he gets milk from my Mom's breast.

He's *always* hungry.
My Dad gives him a bottle sometimes.

My Mom lets me help with the baby's first bath.
He likes it because I am gentle.

I have to be quiet all the time so I don't wake the baby.
That's my Mom looking like an old meany.
I'm not sure I like this baby.

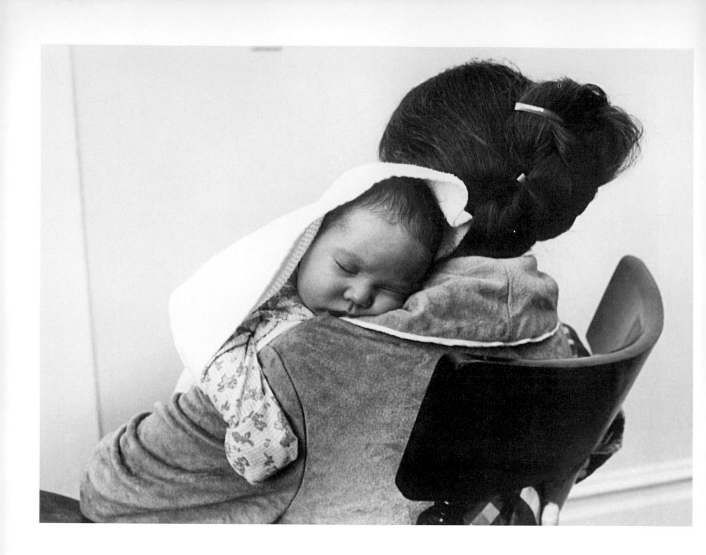

My Mom has to hold him a lot. That makes him happy.
I want her to hold me. That makes me happy.

The baby gets lots of presents. I get to open them.

There is nothing fun for me to play with.

There he is nursing again.
I want my Mom to play with me NOW.

That's me crying. I'm mad.
I don't like the baby.

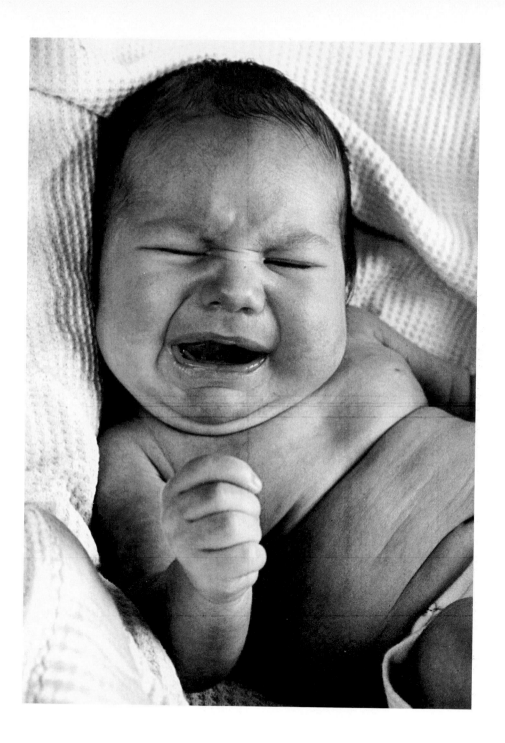

That's the baby crying.
That's what little babies do all the time.

My Mom says she loves me very, very much
and that she can hug us both—even at the same time.

Sometimes she hugs just me.
I like that best of all.

And my Dad tells me he loves me very, very much.

We can still play and roughhouse.

One day my baby smiles at me.

I feel happy.

We play in my room. I show him my toys.
Someday he will be a good friend.
That's what my Mom and Dad tell me.
I think he likes me already.

My friends at school want a baby just like mine.
I tell them they can't have him.

That's my Mom and Dad and me and my baby.
I show my baby how to feed the ducks.
There you are, ducks!

ABOUT THE AUTHOR

Roslyn Banish received a Master's Degree in Photography from the Institute of Design, Chicago. She has taught photography and has exhibited her work in England and the United States.

Ms. Banish currently lives in San Francisco with her husband and two children, where she works as a photographer.

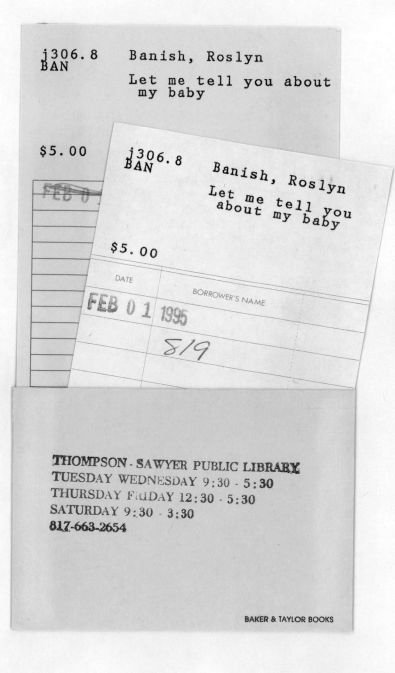